Easy Make & Learn Projects

Penguins

BY DONALD M. SILVER AND PATRICIA J. WYNNE

SCHOLASTIC
PROFESSIONAL BOOKS

NEW YORK • TORONTO • LONDON • AUCKLAND • SYDNEY
MEXICO CITY • NEW DELHI • HONG KONG

For all of our animal friends.

Front cover and interior design by Kathy Massaro
Cover photographs by Donnelly Marks
Cover and interior artwork by Patricia J. Wynne

ISBN: 0-439-04089-2
Copyright © 1999 by Donald M. Silver and Patricia J. Wynne
All rights reserved.
Printed in the U.S.A

Contents

Introduction

What's Inside

Welcome to Penguins! The 15 models in this book will take you and your students on a fun journey into the world of these fascinating birds. Each model focuses on a particular penguin topic. Featured within each chapter are the following sections:

Model Illustration
This picture, labeled with the model's name, shows how the finished model looks. It can be helpful to use as a reference when making the model.

Penguin Particulars
Background information on the chapter's topic and concepts are contained here. Use some or all of this information with the Teaching With the Model section, depending on the level of your students.

Making the Model
These are easy-to-follow instructions with diagrams for assembling the models. See the helpful hints for following the instructions, right.

Teaching With the Model
This section provides a step-by-step lesson map with discussion questions for using the models to teach the chapter's main concepts.

Dive Deeper!
In this section you'll find related activities to extend your students' investigation of the topic.

Helpful Hints for Model-Making

- The thickest black lines on the reproducible pages are CUT lines.
- Dotted lines on the reproducible pages are FOLD lines.
- Some models have slits or windows to cut out. An easy way to make them is to fold the paper at a right angle to the solid cut lines. Then snip along the lines from the crease of the fold inward.

- Often glue sticks can be substituted for tape. However, some situations, for example, creating flaps, require tape.
- If students will be coloring the models and using tape, have them color first so they won't have to color over the tape.
- Some models are more difficult to assemble than others. Read through each Making the Model section (or make the model yourself) beforehand to determine if it's appropriate for your students to do on their own. You can choose to make a more challenging model yourself and use it as a classroom demonstration tool.
- If possible, enlarge the pattern pages to make the models easier for students to assemble.
- If a single model will be handled a great deal, consider creating it from heavier paper. Simply paste the reproducible page onto construction paper before beginning assembly.

Penguin Peek-Through Mask

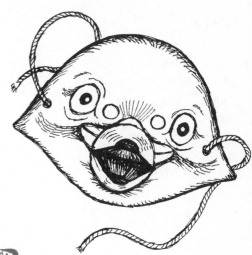

Children make a penguin mask and begin their discovery of penguins.

Penguin Particulars

Penguins are the largest group of flightless birds in the world. Like all birds, penguins have wings, are covered in feathers, lay eggs, and are warm-blooded because they produce and regulate their own body heat. Their torpedo-shaped bodies, powerful short legs with webbed feet, and flipperlike wings make these aquatic birds superb swimmers. Penguins live in large groups along the cooler waters of the Southern Hemisphere, where they hunt for fish and other sea animals. They spend much of their time in the water, but breed, nest, and raise their young on land.

Penguin populations are very vulnerable to human activity. Overfishing depletes their food supply, spilled oil can damage their feathers, and coastal development takes away their nesting areas. Even though most penguins are protected and are no longer hunted for food or oil, more than half of all penguin species are considered endangered or vulnerable.

 ## Making the Model

Materials

* reproducible pages 7–8
* scissors
* tape
* two 10-inch lengths of string or yarn
* sharpened pencil
* crayons, colored pencils, or markers (optional)

1 Photocopy pages 7–8. Color the mask and the beak, if desired. (Choose a penguin type to depict and use the poster on pages 11–13 as a coloring guide.) Cut out the mask along the solid black lines. Cut out the two peek-through holes. Adjust the size of these holes, as needed

2 Place a piece of tape over the small circle at each side of the mask. Use a hole punch or pencil to make a hole through both circles.

Note

Page 8 is a three-dimensional beak that attaches to the mask on page 7. If you'd like to create the masks without the beak, do not photocopy page 8 and stop after step 3.

3 Run one end of the string through each hole and knot at the back of the mask. The ends will tie together to hold the mask on.

4 Cut out the two beak pieces on page 8 along the solid black lines. Fold the upper beak piece along its dotted lines. Slide the upper beak fold under the other fold until they overlap, and tape. Repeat for the lower beak, folding its tab up.

5 Set the lower beak on the mask so that the curved end of the cone just covers the tip of the beak on the mask. Tape down the tab. Tape down the rounded sides of the cone, as shown.

6 Set the upper beak on the mask so that its straight edge meets the straight edge of the lower beak. Tape down the rounded sides of the cone, as in step 5. The beak will open slightly.

Penguin Sightings
• • •

If there is a zoo or conservation park nearby with a penguin exhibit, arrange a class visit. Invite your students to wear their masks on the trip! Or check your local library or video store for a film that features penguins. For Internet "field trips," see Resources, inside back cover, for web sites about penguins.

Teaching With the Model

1 What kind of animal is a penguin? (bird)

❋ How are penguins like other birds? (have feathers, have two feet, lay eggs, and produce their own body heat)

❋ How are penguins different from most other birds? (can't fly; wings are short, stiff, and flipperlike.)

2 Invite students to put on their masks. Challenge them to name ways a penguin might use its beak. List them on the board. (breathe, catch food, take care of its feathers, pick up pebbles or sticks, feed chicks, and defend itself)

3 Do people hurt penguins? (Penguins are rarely hunted by people anymore. However, people put penguins in danger by overfishing waters where penguins hunt, by building on their nesting sites, and by causing oil spills which in turn cause serious harm to penguins' feathers. Ask students how people can help penguins. (conservation laws, limits on fish catches, setting aside areas as parks, and so on.)

Penguin Mask
(Basic Pattern)

Cut out

Cut out

Penguin Mask
(Beak Pattern)

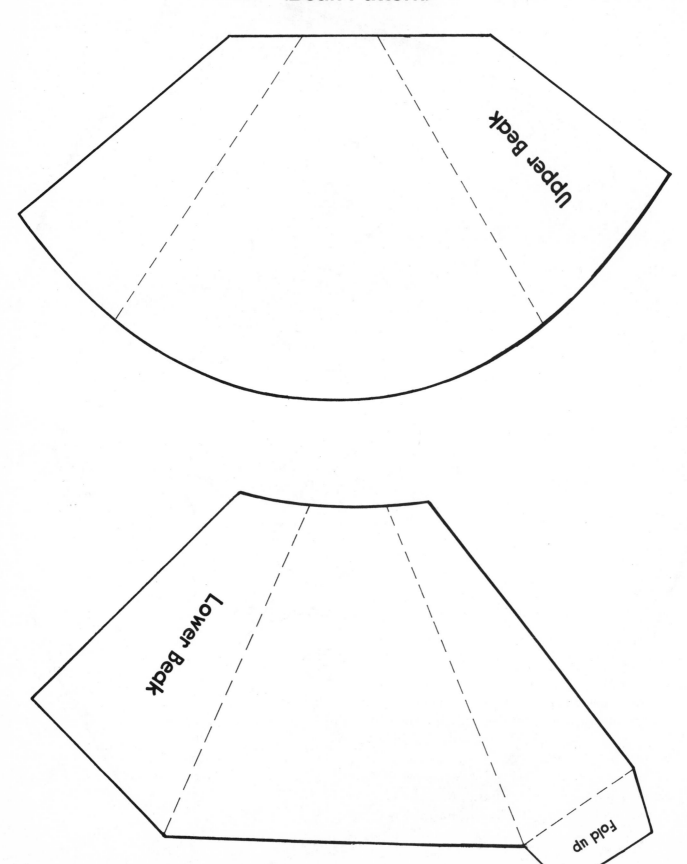

Upper Beak

Lower Beak

Fold up

8

Easy Make & Learn Projects: Penguins   Scholastic Professional Books

Color-by-Number Penguin Poster

Children make a color-by-number poster to become familiar with the 17 different types of penguins.

Penguin Particulars

Penguins are a family of birds that includes 17 different kinds, or species. They are: emperor, king, gentoo, Adélie, chinstrap, African, Galápagos, Humboldt, Magellanic, erect-crested, fiordland, macaroni, rockhopper, royal, Snares Island, yellow-eyed, and little blue.

All penguins share the traits of being flightless and having flipper-like wings, webbed feet, insulating fat, and short feathers. But penguins vary greatly in size and other identifying characteristics. The largest penguin, the emperor, can stand more than 42 inches (105 cm) high and weigh 65 pounds (30 kg). In contrast, little blue penguins are only 12 to 15 inches (30 to 37.5 cm) tall and weigh only about 2.2 pounds (1 kg).

Penguins are known for their "tuxedo" coloration of dark on the back and white on the breast. But the little blue and emperor penguins are actually more gray than black, and the Magellanic, African, and Galápagos penguins have dark stripes and splotches on their flanks, throats, and heads. Yellow-eyed, rockhopper, royal, and other penguins also have distinguishing plumes of bright yellow head feathers.

Making the Model

1 Photocopy pages 11–13 onto white paper. Cut pages 12 and 13 along the solid black lines.

2 Lightly glue the edge of page 12 to page 11 as shown. Turn over and secure with tape on the back. Repeat to attach page 13 to page 12.

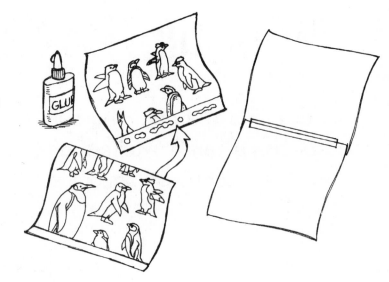

3 Color the poster by number, using the color key at the bottom of the poster. Areas that are not numbered should remain white. Note: Students will use their posters as a reference for coloring the penguins on future models.

Teaching With the Model

1 Ask students how many kinds, or species, of penguins there are. (17) Invite them to count the penguins on the poster.

2 Ask your students to look carefully at their posters and point out colors and markings that will help them tell one kind of penguin from another. For example, macaroni penguins look like they have bushy eyebrows; yellow-eyeds have yellow eyes; chinstraps have a thin black line under their chins, and so on.

3 Encourage students to name the characteristics while you list them on the board. Let students work in groups to come up with ways to group the 17 species based on shared characteristics.

4 Are all the penguins on the poster the same size? (no) Invite students to write the size of the largest penguin (emperor, 42 inches tall and 65 pounds) and the smallest penguin (little blue, 12–15 inches tall and 2.2 pounds) on their posters. Consider asking students to research the size of the other penguins and add the information to their posters.

Materials

❄ reproducible pages 11–13
❄ glue
❄ tape
❄ crayons, colored pencils, or markers

Dive Deeper!

Penguin Flash Cards

• ● ●

Create flash cards using the 17 penguins on pages 11–13. Have students color and cut out the penguins and then paste or tape them onto index cards. Tell students to write the name of each penguin on the back of its card. Let students use the cards to learn the names and identifying characteristics of the different penguins.

Color-by-Number Penguins

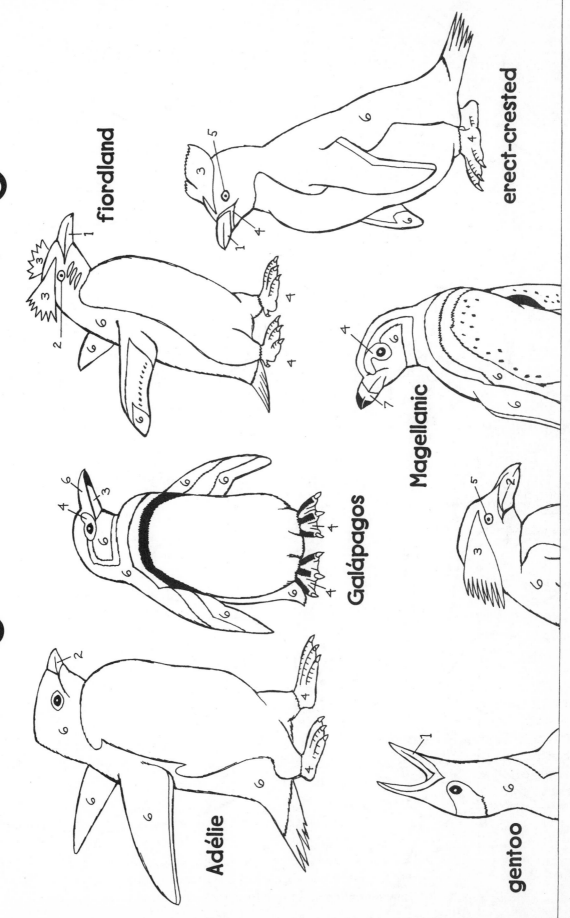

fiordland

erect-crested

Magellanic

Galápagos

Adélie

gentoo

Glue edge of page 12 here.

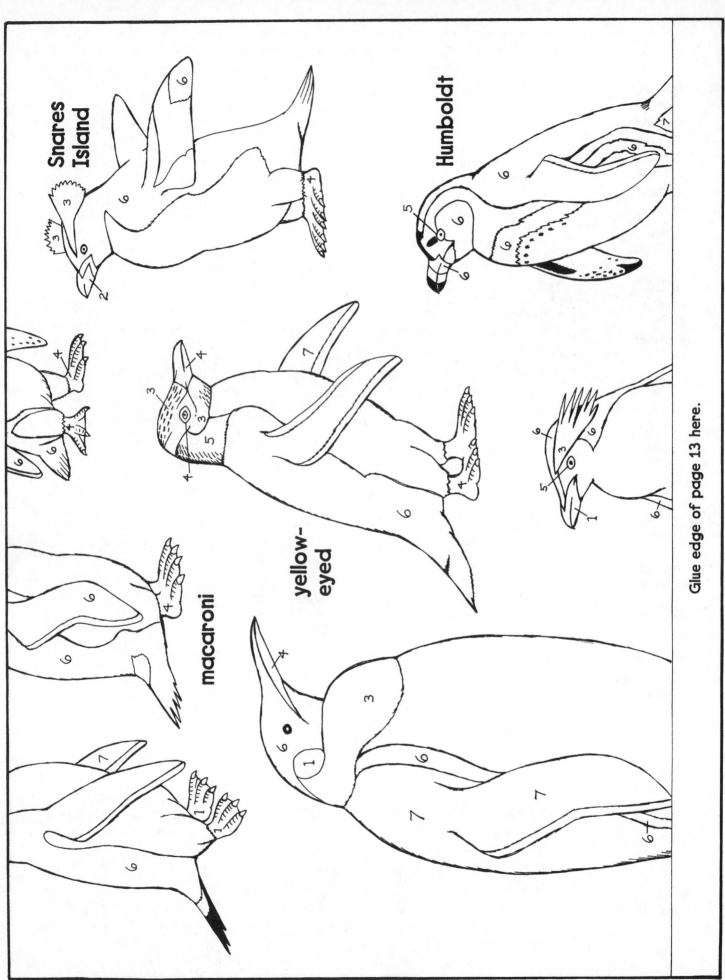

Snares Island

Humboldt

macaroni

yellow-
eyed

Glue edge of page 13 here.

Easy Make & Learn Projects: Penguins

Scholastic Professional Books

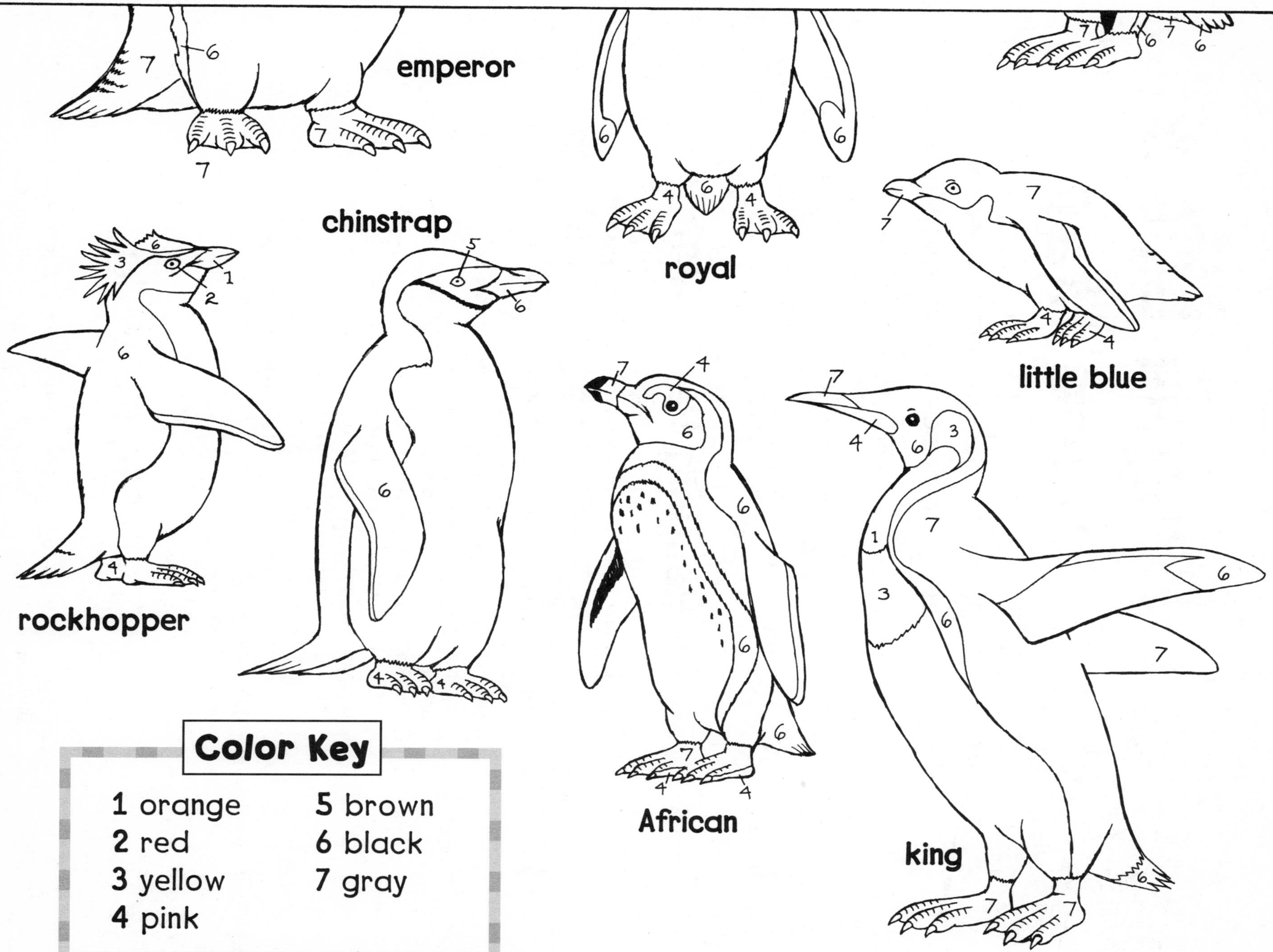

little blue

king

royal

African

emperor

chinstrap

rockhopper

Color Key

1 orange
2 red
3 yellow
4 pink
5 brown
6 black
7 gray

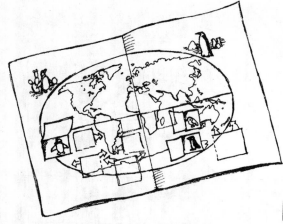

Penguin Lift & Look Map

Children make a map with flaps that lets them discover where penguins live around the world.

Penguin Particulars

Penguins are Southern Hemisphere birds; all 17 kinds live south of the equator. Penguins are famous inhabitants of frigid Antarctica, but some penguins also live along the warm sandy shores of Peru and the Galápagos Islands as well as around the coasts of southern Africa, New Zealand, and Australia. But regardless of the air temperature, all penguins live near cool waters. Cooler waters are more nutrient-rich and support penguin food. Currents carry cold waters north from Antarctica up the coast of South America as well as around Africa, Australia, and New Zealand, where penguins hunt.

Gentoo, chinstrap, Adélie, emperor, macaroni, king, and rockhopper penguins live in the Antarctic region, which includes the surrounding ice sheet and nearby islands. But only emperor and Adélie penguins breed on the frozen continent itself. It is a harsh environment, nearly completely covered in ice that never melts. In places the ice is more than a mile thick and winter temperatures reach -76°F (-60°C) with winds of 125 miles (200 km) per hour.

Materials

❄ reproducible pages 16–18
❄ scissors
❄ tape
❄ crayons, colored pencils, or markers (optional)

Making the Model

1 Photocopy pages 16–18. Color the penguins as well as the oceans and continents on the pages, if desired. Use the penguin poster on pages 11–13 as a coloring guide.

2 Cut the right-hand border off page 16 along the outer solid lines. Tape the edge of page 16 along the solid black line on page 17. This is the map page.

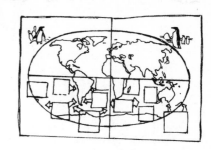

3 Cut the penguin page (page 18) in half along the solid black lines.

4 Cut open each of the 11 flaps on the map page along their three solid black lines. Do not cut along the dotted lines. (See page 4 for cutting tips.)

5 Place penguin page A on the left and page B on the right. Place the map pages on top of the penguin pages. Line up the penguins with the flaps and tape the pages together along the edges in a number of places.

Teaching With the Model

1 Point out the continents on a classroom globe. Focus on Antarctica and its position relative to South America, Africa, Australia, and New Zealand. Point out the equator and explain that it is an imaginary line that divides the northern half of the earth from the southern half. Invite students to read their maps and lift the flaps. Ask questions to check their understanding of the map, such as:

❄ Do any penguins live above the equator? (no) Which penguin lives the farthest north? (Galápagos)

❄ Which penguins live on or near New Zealand? (erect-crested, fiordland, Snares Island, yellow-eyed, and royal) Which live off Africa? (African) On Australian islands? (little blue)

❄ Which penguins live on or near Antarctica? (emperor and Adélie penguins live on Antarctica; gentoo, king, rockhopper, chinstrap, and macaroni penguins live around it) What is Antarctica like? (cold, icy, and barren)

2 Show students where they live on the globe and invite them to mark their home on their maps with an X. Ask: Which penguins live closest to you?

Dive Deeper!

Map Matching

Photocopy pages 16 and 17 and cut out the continents. Place Antarctica in the center. Using a globe as a reference, arrange the continents around Antarctica. Then photocopy the penguins on page 18, cut them out, and challenge children to place the penguins on top of the continents where they live using the LIFT & LOOK MAP as a guide.

Where Do Pen

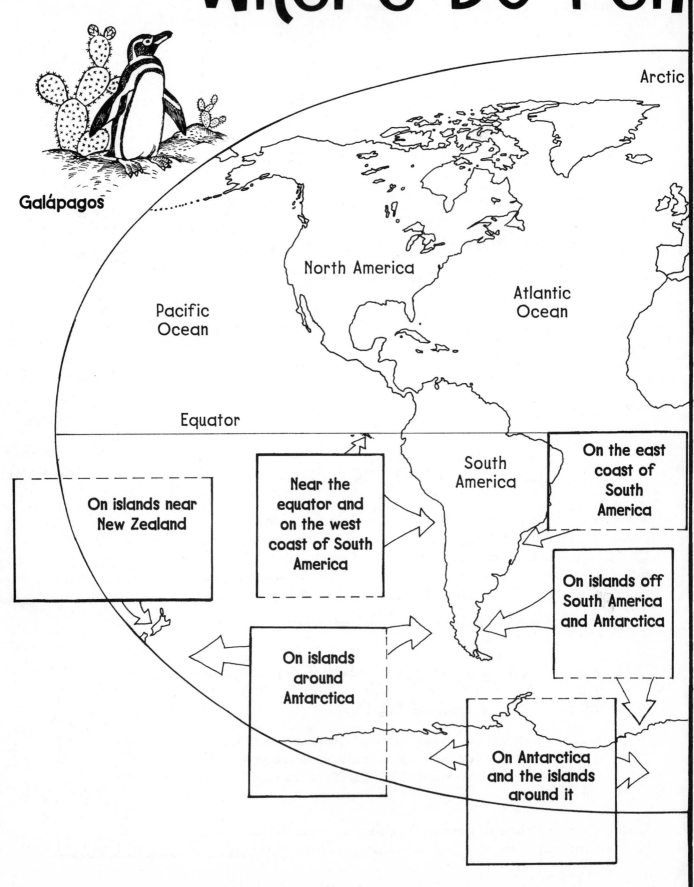

Galápagos

Arctic

North America

Pacific Ocean

Atlantic Ocean

Equator

South America

On the east coast of South America

On islands near New Zealand

Near the equator and on the west coast of South America

On islands off South America and Antarctica

On islands around Antarctica

On Antarctica and the islands around it

guins Live?

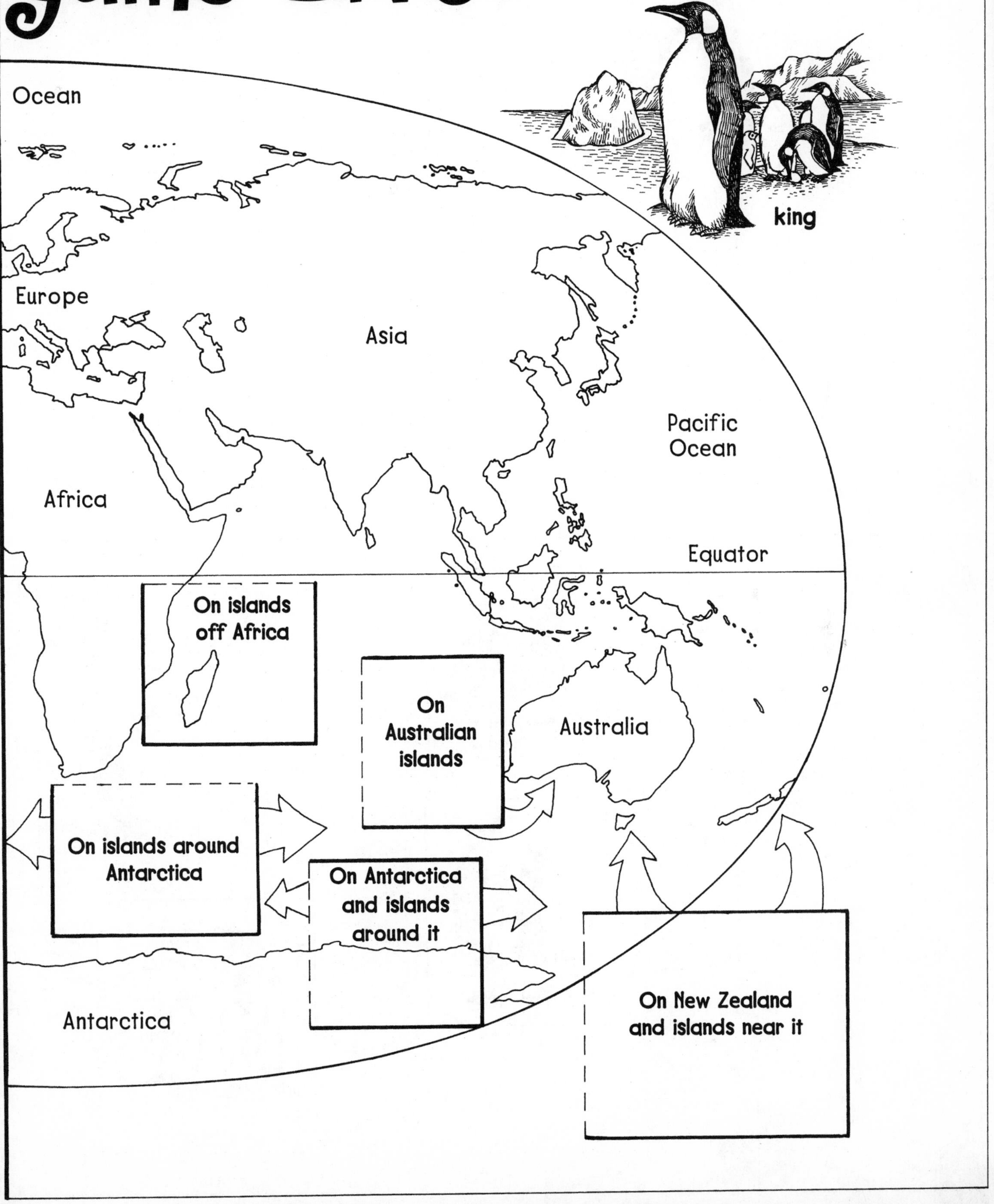

Ocean

king

Europe

Asia

Africa

Pacific
Ocean

Equator

On islands
off Africa

On
Australian
islands

Australia

On islands around
Antarctica

On Antarctica
and islands
around it

On New Zealand
and islands near it

Antarctica

Penguin Lift & Look Map

fiordland, yellow-eyed, Snares Island & royal

macaroni

chinstrap

little blue

African

B

A

erect-crested

Humboldt &
Galápagos

Magellanic

rockhopper

gentoo & king

emperor
& Adélie

Easy Make & Learn Projects: Penguins

Scholastic Professional Books

Penguin Parts Mini-Book

Children make a penguin-shaped mini-book that helps them investigate what's inside a penguin's body.

Penguin Parts

Penguin Particulars

The body of a penguin is well adapted to its cold-water environment. Penguins are covered in short, oily top feathers that form a waterproof coat. Penguins care for these feathers by preening—they use their beaks to spread oil from a gland at the base of their tail over the feathers to keep them waterproof and bendable. Underneath the top feathers is fluffy down that traps a layer of warm air against their skin. Under the skin is a thick layer of fat, called blubber, that keeps body heat in and cold out.

Penguins do not have hollow lightweight bones like flying birds. The solid heavier bones of penguins help keep them underwater when swimming and diving. A penguin's wing bones are joined together to form a strong, stiff paddle, and they have powerful muscles attached to them. Their wings act as paddles that push water and propel them forward. A penguin's streamlined torpedo shape allows it to move quickly through the water. Their webbed feet and tail help them steer while swimming.

Materials

* reproducible pages 21–22
* scissors
* tape
* glue
* crayons, colored pencils, or markers (optional)

Making the Model

1. Make double-sided copies of pages 21–22, or glue the two pages together. Check that the cover and page 2 are back to back.

2 Color the pages, if desired. The penguin shown is a Humboldt. Use the penguin poster on pages 11–13 as a coloring guide.

3 Cut the page in half along the solid black horizontal center line.

4 Fold each half along the dotted vertical line so that the cover and page 5 are on top.

5 Place the cover through page 4 on top of pages 5 to 8. Tape together on the left along the dotted line to make the book's binding.

6 Cut the top off the entire book along the solid black line on the cover.

Dive Deeper!

Why It's Waxy

· · ·

The waterproofing oil that penguins spread on their feathers is waxy. Help your students understand how a waxy oil coating waterproofs: Take two pieces of paper and draw a small circle on each. Color in one of the circles with a wax crayon. Next, sprinkle some water on each circle and hold up both sheets of paper. Ask: What happens? (The water will soak into the uncolored circle but run off the crayon-colored circle.)

Teaching With the Model

1 Let students read their mini-books. Then ask: How do penguins stay warm? (They have feathers that keep out water and trap warm air next to the skin, and they have a layer of insulating fat called blubber.)

2 Why does a penguin need large, strong muscles? (to move its flipperlike wings up and down when swimming)

3 Are penguin bones lightweight or heavy? (heavy) Do you think all birds have heavy bones? (No, most birds that fly have lightweight, hollow bones.)

4 What are some of the soft parts (organs) of a penguin's body? (brain, heart, lungs, crop, intestines) Review the function of each organ. (The brain is the body's control center; the heart pumps blood throughout the body; the lungs enable the penguin to breathe; the crop is a pouch in the throat where food is partially digested; the intestines further break down food so that it can be used by the body.)

5 How does a penguin's body help it swim? (Its streamlined shape moves quickly through water, its wings act as paddles that push water, and its webbed feet help the penguin steer.)

Scholastic Professional Books

A penguin's muscles
are strong.

④

Penguin Parts

---

⑦

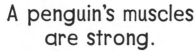

A penguin's shape
helps it swim.
So do its flippers and
webbed feet.

⑥ Under the bones are many
soft parts called organs.

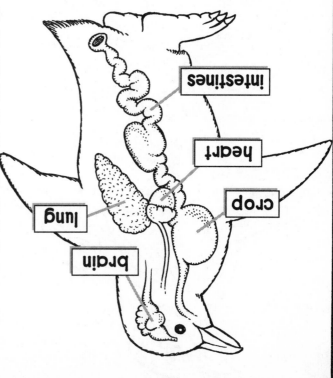

intestines

heart

crop

lung

brain

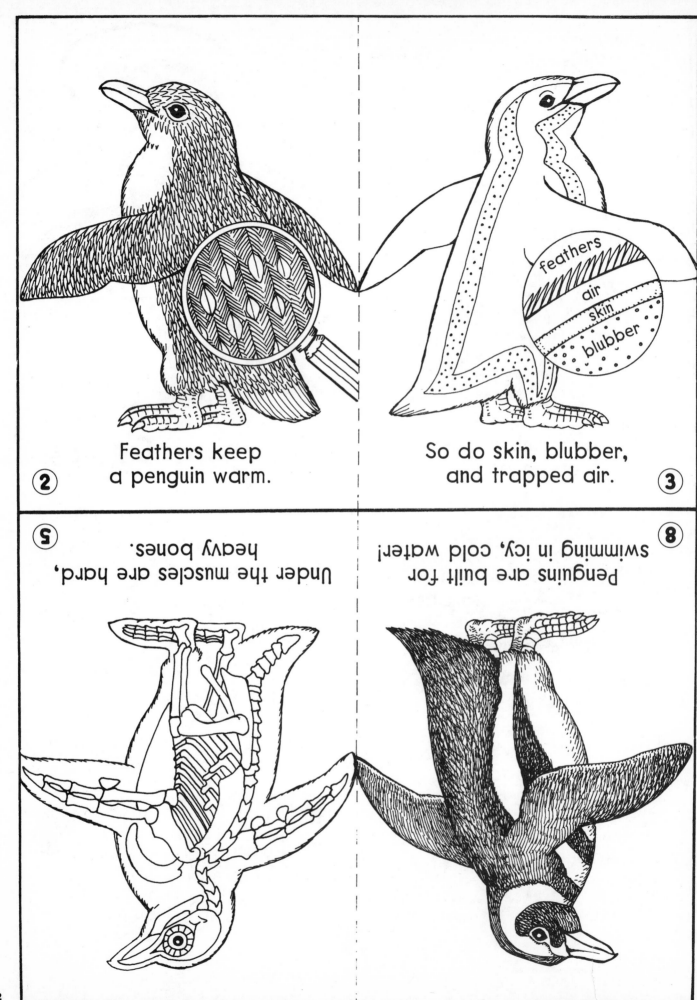

Feathers keep
a penguin warm.

(2)

So do skin, blubber,
and trapped air.

(3)

feathers
air
skin
blubber

Under the muscles are hard,
heavy bones.

(5)

Penguins are built for
swimming in icy, cold water!

(8)

22

Leapin' Penguins Wheel

This wheel helps children understand how penguins breathe while swimming.

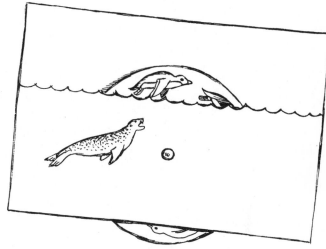

Penguin Particulars

Air-breathing penguins must carry air in their lungs when they dive and swim. When swimming underwater, a penguin will leap into the air to quickly catch its breath. This is called porpoising. Besides being a quick way to get air, porpoising can allow penguins to quickly change direction or confuse and escape a predator when they dive back in.

 ## Making the Model

1 Photocopy page 25. Color the page, if desired. The penguins shown are Adélies. Use the penguin poster on pages 11–13 as a coloring guide. The seal is a leopard seal. This type of seal is gray to brown.

Materials

- ❄ reproducible page 25
- ❄ scissors
- ❄ sharpened pencil
- ❄ brass fastener
- ❄ colored pencils, crayons, or markers (optional)

2 Cut out the rectangular piece along the solid black lines. Set the rectangle aside. Cut out the circle on the lower half, and punch out the center circle with a sharpened pencil.

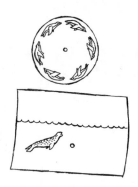

3 Cut the water surface along the heavy black line on the rectangular piece. Use a sharpened pencil to punch out its center hole.

4 Place the circle behind the rectangular piece. Slide the top of the circle up through the cut section of the water, as shown.

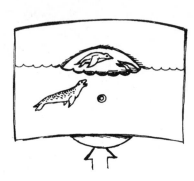

5 Insert the fastener through the two center holes and bend back its ends.

Teaching With the Model

1 Begin by asking: How do penguins breathe? (Penguins breathe air with lungs.) Can they breathe underwater? (No, they are not like fish. Penguins must hold their breath while they swim underwater.)

2 What happens when penguins run out of air underwater? (They have to come to the surface.)

3 Invite students to turn the wheel on their models to make the penguins leap, or porpoise. Ask: How do you think penguins come up for air? (They speed up and then leap out of the water, take a deep breath to refill their lungs, and dive back in.)

4 Direct students' attention to the hungry leopard seal, a penguin predator. Ask: How else might leaping help penguins? (It can help a penguin escape a predator by confusing it.)

Leapin' Penguins

Turn the wheel.

Watch the penguins leap out of the water.

They take deep breaths.

When penguins dive back into the water, they swim away fast from enemies!

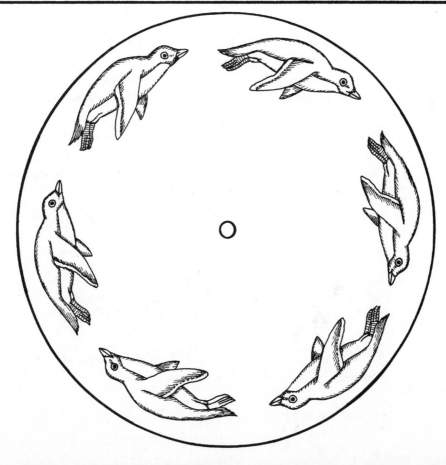

Leapin' Penguins Wheel

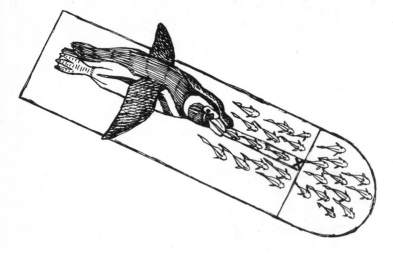

On-the-Hunt Slider

Children make a model
to help them understand
how penguins swim
to catch food.

Penguin Particulars

Penguins are superb swimmers. A penguin swims by beating its stiff flipper-like wings and then gliding along—it flies underwater! Most penguins swim at speeds of 5 to 10 miles per hour (8 to 16 km per hour). Penguins swim to travel back and forth between nesting areas and feeding grounds, which can be many miles out to sea. They must also swim and dive to catch food for themselves and for their chicks, as well as to escape leopard seals, killer whales, and other penguin predators. When a penguin spots a meal, it swims toward it, grabs it with its beak, and swallows it. Stiff spines in a penguin's mouth help it grip slippery prey.

Materials

* reproducible pages 28-29
* scissors
* tape
* 4- by 14-inch sheet of blue paper (optional)
* crayons, colored pencils, or markers (optional)

Making the Model

1 Photocopy pages 28–29. Color the pages, if desired. The penguin shown is a Magellanic. Use the penguin poster on pages 11–13 as a coloring guide.

2 Cut out the four pieces on page 28 along the solid black outer lines.

3 On the rectangular piece, starting at the X, cut the thin strip on both sides along the solid black line, as shown.

4 Cut out the penguin on page 29. (Set aside the remaining piece and use it with the lesson on page 30.) Cut along the short solid black lines marked A and B on each penguin half.

5 Fold the penguin along the dotted lines. Fold down the tab on wing A, slide it into the slot marked A, and tape from behind. Repeat for wing B. Tape the penguin closed at the top, as shown.

6 Slide the penguin over the strip as far back as it can go. Be sure its head faces the X.

7 Tape the rounded end piece to the X end of the model. The tape should cover the free end of the strip to anchor it.

8 Tape the entire finished model to a sheet of paper for added strength, if desired.

Teaching With the Model

1 Ask: Why do penguins swim? (travel to nesting sites, hunt for food, escape predators) What does a penguin use to swim? (Its wings—it beats them and then glides along.)

2 Invite children to move their penguin along the strip on their ON THE HUNT model so it can snatch up the fish on the model. Ask: How does a penguin catch food? (It swims toward it, grabs it with its beak, and swallows it.)

On-the-Hunt Slider

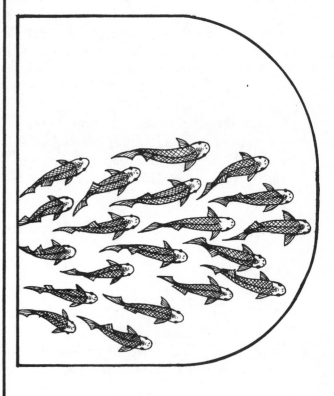

ON THE HUNT

Swim Magellanic penguin.
Catch lots of fish.
Your chick at home is hungry.
It is waiting for food.

X

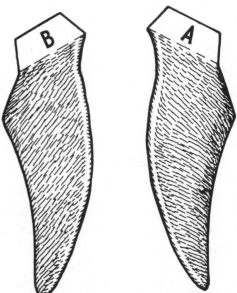

B

A

Easy Make & Learn Projects: Penguins   Scholastic Professional Books

On-the-Hunt Slider

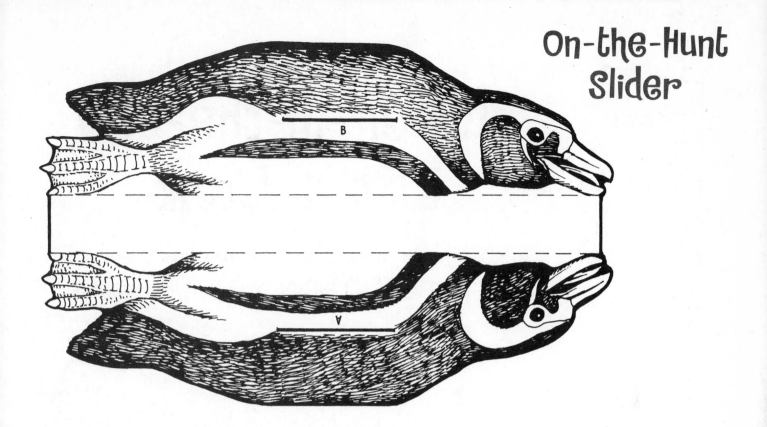

Supper-in-the-Sea Lift & Look

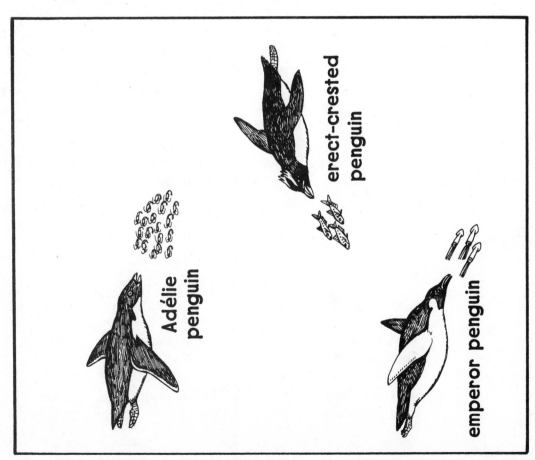

erect-crested penguin

Adélie penguin

emperor penguin

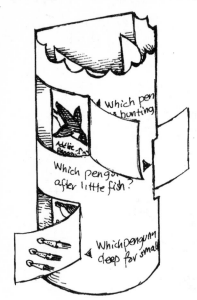

Supper-in-the-sea Lift & Look

Children make a model that lets them discover what different penguins like to eat.

Penguin Particulars

Penguins eat small fishes and squids, and crabs and other crustaceans such as tiny shrimplike krill. Each kind of penguin prefers certain kinds of food but will eat whatever it can find when hungry.

The animals that penguins hunt live in different levels of the sea. Krill live near the surface; sardines, crabs, and other small fishes live in deeper waters; and squids live in even deeper waters. Penguins can dive deeper and stay underwater longer than any other bird. Most penguins dive less than 230 feet (69 m) after food, though a king penguin can dive 1000 feet (300 m) or more to hunt squid. Most penguins stay underwater for a minute or two and then surface to breathe before diving again.

Materials

* reproducible pages 29 and 32-33
* scissors
* tape
* crayons, colored pencils, or markers (optional)

 ## Making the Model

1 Make copies of pages 32-33, and glue the two pages together back to back. Color these pages, if desired.

2 Cut off the top along the solid black "water" line. Cut open the flaps on three sides along the solid black lines on page 32. (See cutting tips on page 4.)

3 Photocopy the bottom portion of page 29. Cut out the box (with the pictures of penguins) along the solid black lines. Color, if desired. Use the penguin poster on pages 11–13 as a coloring guide.

4 Place the double-sided page so that the blank section is on top, as shown. Fold along the dotted line. Then crease well, open out, and smooth flat.

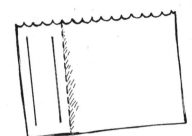

5 Tape the penguin piece to the two tape lines, as shown.

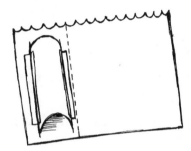

6 Wrap the right edge of the sheet around and tape the three nonflap sections to the back where indicated.

Teaching With the Model

1 Ask: What do penguins eat? (small fishes, small squids, and crabs and other tiny crustaceans such as krill)

2 Invite children to read the questions on their model and then open the flaps and find out the answers.

3 Which penguin hunts near the surface of the sea? Which penguin dives the deepest for food?

Dive Deeper!

Mobile Food

• ■ •

Invite students to make a mobile of the penguins and foods featured on the SUPPER-IN-THE-SEA LIFT & LOOK model. Photocopy page 32 and the penguins box on page 29. Color and then cut out the penguins and the sea creatures. Have students tape yarn to each and attach them to a hanger as a mobile. Challenge students to hang each of the penguins near the food it prefers and at levels that represent the ocean depths where the prey live.

Supper-in-the-Sea Lift & Look

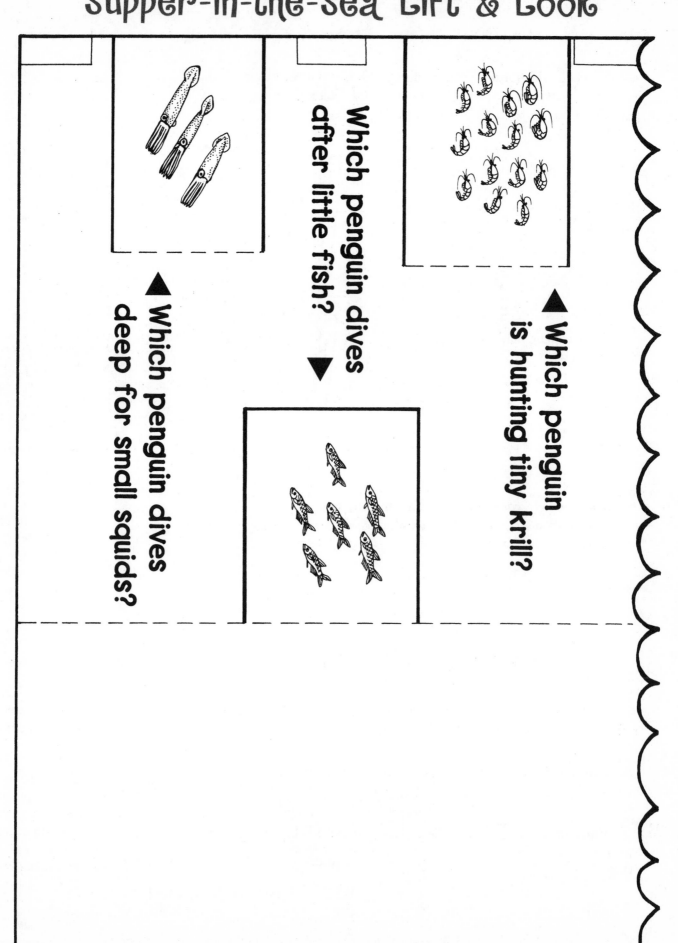

▲ Which penguin
is hunting tiny krill?

▼ Which penguin dives
after little fish?

▲ Which penguin dives
deep for small squids?

Easy Make & Learn Projects: Penguins

Scholastic Professional Books

Supper-in-the-Sea Lift & Look

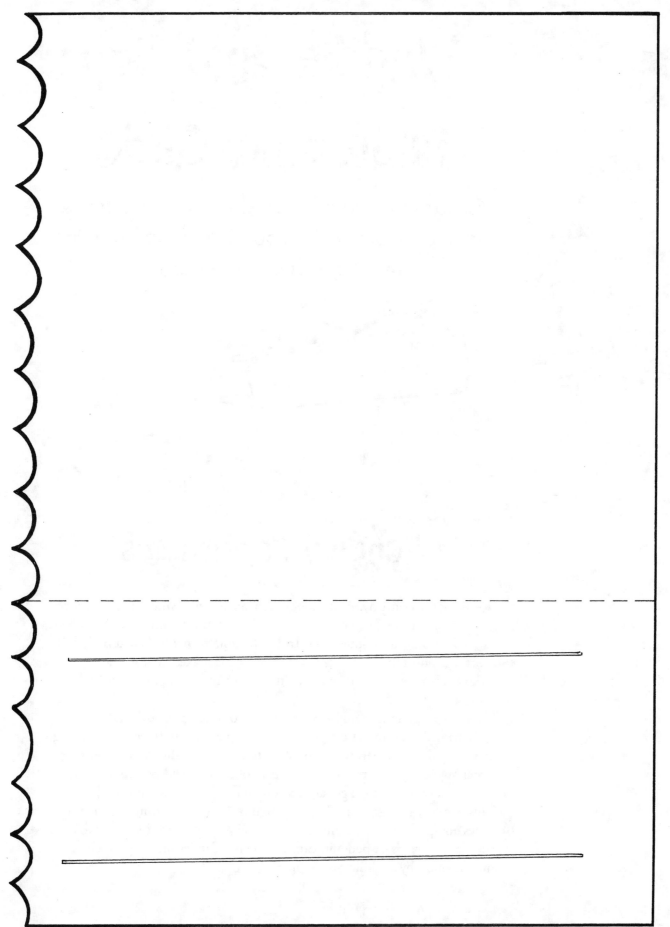

Waddle and Hop
✳ ✳ ✳
Slide and Glide

Children make models that illustrate three ways penguins get around on land: hopping, waddling, and tobogganing.

Penguin Particulars

Penguins can't fly. And though they are expert swimmers and most at home in the sea, penguins must also get around on land. A penguin isn't built for taking long strides. Its long torpedo-shaped body has short legs positioned far back on its body. This makes their gait an awkward waddle. They may look clumsy, but most penguins can walk about as fast as a person.

Many penguins also hop to climb slopes or cross over rocky areas. The aptly named rockhopper penguin can hop up a slope 400 feet (120 m) high by taking short hops from one boulder to another. If the slope is too steep, a rockhopper can grasp a rock with its hooked beak and pull itself up.

A third way penguins get around on land is by sliding on their bellies. This is called tobogganing. First a penguin flops on its stomach, then it slides and glides along on the ice and snow pushing with its feet and paddle-like wings. A penguin can toboggan for miles, moving much faster than it could by waddling or hopping.

Making the Models

Waddle and Hop

Materials

❄ reproducible page 36
❄ 4-inch square of construction paper
❄ scissors
❄ tape
❄ 4- by 8-inch strip of paper
❄ crayons, colored pencils, or markers (optional)

1 Photocopy page 36. Color the two rockhopper penguins, if desired. Use the penguin poster on pages 11–13 as a coloring guide.

2 Cut out both double penguins along the solid black outer lines.

3 Fold each penguin in half along the dotted line on top of its head.

4 Fold the flap and tab along the dotted lines under the penguin's feet.

5 Tape the bottom flap, as shown, to give each penguin a stable base.

6 Tape the WADDLE penguin's base to both ends of the construction paper square, as shown. The paper will make a rocker.

7 Fold the 4- by 8-inch strip of construction paper into an accordion, with each fold about 1 1/2 inches wide.

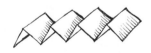

8 Tape the HOP penguin onto the top fold. Then tape the top two folds of the accordion together as shown.

Waddle and Hop

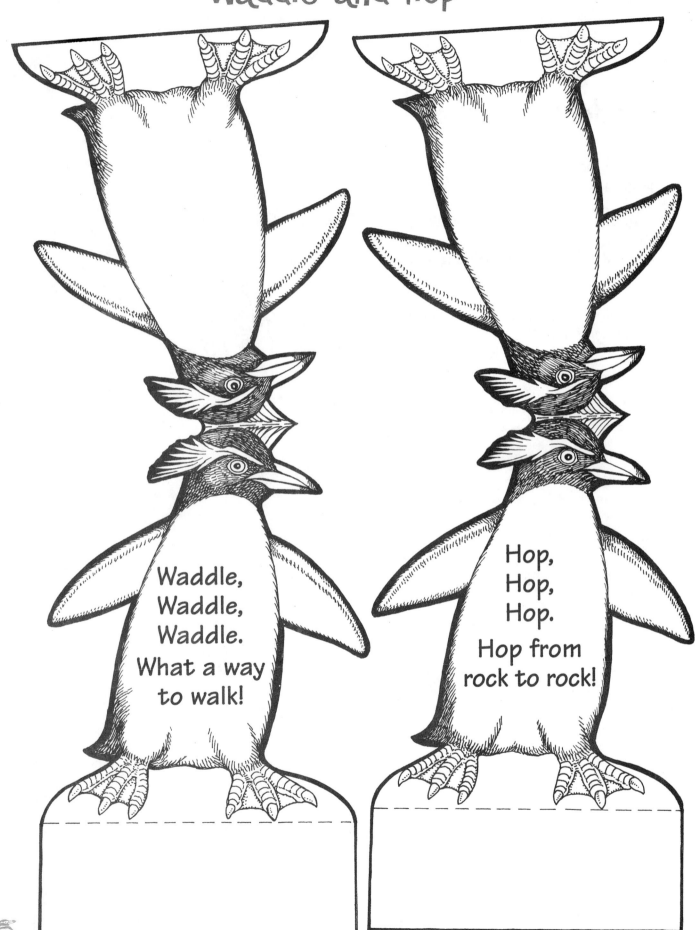

Waddle,
Waddle,
Waddle.
What a way
to walk!

Hop,
Hop,
Hop.
Hop from
rock to rock!

Easy Make & Learn Projects: Penguins Scholastic Professional Books

Slide and Glide

1 Photocopy page 38. Color the sliding Adélie penguins, if desired. Use the penguin poster on pages 11–13 as a coloring guide.

2 Cut out the three pieces along the solid black lines.

3 Fold the penguin piece along the dotted lines and tape it together at the top to make a triangular tube.

4 Place the thin strip piece over the shaded band on the big piece. Tape the strip down at one end as shown.

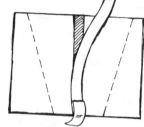

5 Fold the big piece along the dotted lines. Push the folds together until they touch, and tape at both ends as shown.

6 Slip the penguin piece onto the free end of the taped strip so that the penguins are facing downhill. Tape down the free end of the strip as in step 4.

Teaching With the Models

1 Ask: Can penguins fly? (no) Name some other flightless birds for students, such as ostriches, emus, kiwis, and cassowaries. Ask: How do you think these birds get around? (by walking and running)

2 How do penguins get around on land? (They waddle, hop, and toboggan.)

❋ Invite students to make their HOP penguin models hop by placing two fingers inside the base of the penguin and pressing down and letting go.

❋ Students can make their other penguin waddle by rocking the model back and forth. Which way of getting around would work better on snow? (waddling) Over rocks? (hopping)

❋ Invite students to slide the Adélie penguins down the slope on the SLIDE AND GLIDE model. Ask: When is tobogganing better than hopping or waddling? (on slopes) Ask your students if they've ever gone tobogganing or sledding. What was it like?

Materials

❋ reproducible page 38
❋ scissors
❋ tape
❋ crayons, colored pencils, or markers (optional)

Dive Deeper!

Be a Penguin

Divide the class into three groups, and invite students to wear their penguin masks. (See page 5.) Tell one group to walk around the room or school yard, tell another group to waddle, and tell the third to hop. Which group gets around the quickest? The slowest? What about going up a flight of stairs?

Slide and Glide

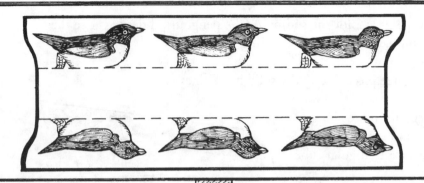

Slide and Glide

When is a penguin like a sled?
When it flops on its belly
and glides, slides, glides!

Off-to-the-Sea/ To-the-Feeding Grounds Dioramas

✳ ✳ ✳

Follow-the-Leaper Pull-Through

Children make three models to help them understand penguin migration.

Penguin Particulars

There is no food for penguins on land, only in the sea. Some penguins—like yellow-eyeds, Galápagos, and Humboldts—find food in the waters near their breeding colonies all year long. Other penguins must travel, or migrate, between rich feeding grounds and their breeding colony. Many penguins, including Adélies and emperors, spend three to seven months of the year at sea feeding between breeding seasons. During this time they fatten up so they can survive the lean breeding season without eating.

Penguins migrate both overland and by sea. In the polar region, areas that are open sea during the summer become solid pack ice during the winter. Groups of penguins will sometimes have to walk many miles just to reach the seashore, leap in, and begin their long swim to rich feeding grounds. Just how penguins find these faraway schools of fish, krill, or squid is unknown.

Penguins face many dangers when migrating. Hungry sea lions or leopard seals lurk between loose ice chunks and wait for penguins to leap into the water. Penguins heading out to sea are especially vulnerable because they are weak from having fasted while on land.

❄ reproducible pages 41–42

❄ scissors

❄ tape

❄ 2 shoe boxes or other small boxes (cereal boxes with a window cut out work well)

❄ two 15-inch lengths of string

❄ crayons, markers, or colored pencils (optional)

Making the Models

Off-to-the-Sea/To-the-Feeding Grounds Dioramas

1 Photocopy pages 41–42. Color the pages, if desired. All the penguins are Adélies. Use the penguin poster on pages 11–13 as a coloring guide.

2 Cut out the three standing penguins on page 41.

3 Set a shoe box on its side. Tape the OFF TO THE SEA piece inside the back of the shoe box.

4 Tape the three standing penguins to the middle of the string, as shown. Space them a half inch or less apart.

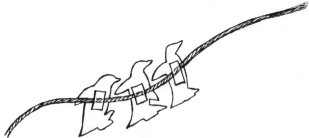

5 Use scissors to cut a small hole on each side of the shoe box about an inch below the text.

6 Thread the ends of the string through the holes and tie a knot in each end. Pull the string so the penguins are at the far right side of the box.

7 Repeat steps 3 to 7 using the TO THE FEEDING GROUNDS piece, another shoe box, another piece of string, and the three swimming penguins.

OFF TO THE SEA

Waddle, waddle, waddle.
It is time for hungry penguins
to fatten up at sea.

Off-to-the-Sea Diorama

41

To-the-Feeding Grounds Diorama

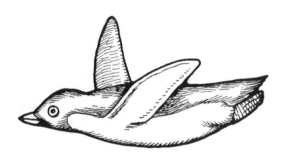

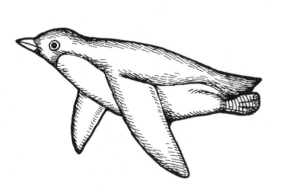

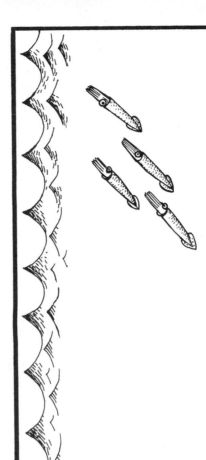

TO THE FEEDING GROUNDS

Paddle, paddle, paddle.
Soon there will be lots of food to eat.

Easy Make & Learn Projects: Penguins

Scholastic Professional Books

Follow-the-Leaper Pull-Through

1 Photocopy page 44. Color the penguins, if desired. All the penguins are Adélies. Use the penguin poster on pages 11–13 as a coloring guide.

2 Cut out the two pieces along the outer solid black lines. Make three slits in the large piece. Cut along the two solid lines and the wavy line.

3 Thread the PULL piece through the cut slits, as shown.

4 Tape the entire piece onto a sheet of paper for added strength, if desired. (Make sure the PULL piece still slides freely.)

Teaching With the Models

1 Many penguins—but not all—must travel away from their colonies during part of the year. Ask students why they might do this. (to find food) What is this kind of seasonal travel called? (migration) Challenge students to name other birds or animals that migrate. (butterflies, other types of birds, whales)

2 Penguins that migrate to rich feeding grounds often travel both overland and by sea to reach them. Invite students to use the models to illustrate the process.

   ❋ First have them pull the string on the OFF TO THE SEA model to show penguins traveling overland. Ask: Is this a fast way to travel? (not very) How else might they travel overland besides walking? (tobogganing)

   ❋ Ask students what happens when the penguins come to the shoreline. Invite them to work the FOLLOW THE LEAPER model by pulling the strip.

   ❋ Swimming is a faster way to travel. Invite students to pull the string on the TO THE FEEDING GROUNDS model to illustrate this stage.

3 Challenge students to name dangers that penguins might encounter during each stage of migration.

Materials

❋ reproducible page 44
❋ scissors
❋ tape
❋ sheet of paper (optional)
❋ crayons, colored pencils, or markers (optional)

Dive Deeper!

Where Do They Go?

Many kinds of birds spend part of the year in one place and the rest hundreds, even thousands of miles away. Check a bird field guide to find a number of birds in your area that migrate. Find out where they go. Invite students to draw pictures of one of the birds in its winter and summer home, or to chart its migratory path on a map.

Follow-the-Leaper Pull-Through

PULL

FOLLOW THE LEAPER
Ready, set, jump!
One penguin leaps into the water
and all the others follow.

Nesting Time Lift & Look

Children make a poster
of penguin nests that shows
how adult penguins
care for their unborn offspring.

Penguin Particulars

Most penguins lay eggs once a year during a breeding season. In the spring, many penguin species travel to and gather in colonies, called rookeries, to nest and lay eggs. Others gather in midwinter, autumn (in the case of emperors), or in the case of many tropical species, breed year-round as long as there's sufficient food. While some penguin rookeries are on the shore, others are inland. Penguins that breed on Antarctica may travel 20 to 50 miles (32 to 80 km) over sea ice to reach their breeding grounds.

All penguins except king and emperors build nests of some sort, and most lay one or two eggs. Once the eggs are laid, the male penguin sits on the eggs so that a patch of his skin without feathers touches the eggs. This brood patch allows heat from his body to keep the eggs warm while the female penguin goes off to sea to hunt. Within a few days or weeks she returns and takes her turn on the eggs, warming them with her own brood patch while the male feeds at sea. King and emperor penguins carry their single egg on top of their feet and cover it with a flap of loose warm skin. King females and males take turns holding the egg while the other hunts at sea, but male emperors hold their egg the entire nine weeks until it hatches. During this time, the male does not eat and loses a great deal of weight.

Materials

- ❄ reproducible pages 49–50
- ❄ scissors
- ❄ tape
- ❄ large sheet of paper (at least 10 by 11 inches)
- ❄ crayons, markers, or colored pencils (optional)

Dive Deeper!

Egg Walk

• • •

Allow children to carry eggs on their feet as emperor and king penguins do. Make eggs out of play dough or clay (or use plastic Easter eggs) and have children take off their shoes. Place an egg on each child's feet and invite children to shuffle around the room. Suggest that they curl their toes to keep the eggs from rolling off. Ask: How would you like the job of egg keeper?

✂ Making the Model

1 Photocopy pages 49–50. Cut off the left-hand section of page 50 and set aside the WHAT'S INSIDE THIS EGG? part. (Use with the lesson on page 47.) Color the pages, if desired. Use the penguin poster on pages 11–13 as a coloring guide.

2 Cut out the text box on page 49 and tape it near the top of the sheet of paper.

3 Cut out the eight pieces from pages 49–50 along the outer solid lines. Cut out the inside of the little blue penguin's nest. Tape each of the three nests and the emperor penguin to the paper, spacing them apart. (Avoid putting tape around the inside of the little blue's nest.)

4 To complete the poster, see Teaching With the Model, below.

Teaching With the Model

1 Find out what students know about penguin reproduction. Ask: Do penguins lay eggs or have live young? (lay eggs) Do they breed year-round or only during a breeding season? (season) Do penguins breed, nest, and raise young alone or in groups? (in groups called colonies, at nesting areas called rookeries)

2 Do penguins build nests? (some do, some don't) What are nests made of? (pebbles, grass, sticks)

3 Invite students to guess how to match the four remaining pieces (two adult penguins, one pair of penguin chicks, and one skin fold) to the correct nest. Then have students tape the pieces in place as follows:

- ❄ Place the gentoo on top of the nest with the chick. Tape the gentoo only at its top, so that the adult makes a flap over the chick.
- ❄ Tape the Adélie penguin next to the stones.
- ❄ Slide the pair of little blue penguins inside the cutout portion of their nest and tape.
- ❄ Place the emperor skin fold over its egg and tape to make a flap, as with the gentoo.

4 Check for understanding by asking:

- ❄ What is an Adélie's nest made of? (small stones)
- ❄ What is a little blue's nest made of? (grass and sticks)
- ❄ What is a gentoo's nest made of? (a hole in the ground, lined with grass)
- ❄ Does an emperor penguin build a nest? (No, the male holds the egg on its feet and covers it with a warm flap of skin.)

What's Inside This Egg?
Peek & Learn

Children make a model
of a penguin egg
to get a close-up look
at how a penguin chick
develops.

What's Inside This Egg?
Open it and see.
It is a penguin chick.
You helped it hatch!

Penguin Particulars

All the components necessary for a chick to develop are housed inside the egg laid by the mother penguin. Inside its strong, protective shell, a penguin embryo grows from a tiny egg cell on the yolk, which provides it with nutrition. Surrounding the yolk is the albumen, which cushions the embryo and supplies protein and water. Tiny pores in the eggshell allow oxygen, carbon dioxide, and water vapor to pass through. This exchange of gases is necessary for healthy embryonic development. As the embryo grows, it also uses calcium from the shell to help its bones develop. By the time the chick is ready to hatch, the eggshell has thinned.

Small penguins, such as little blues and Adélies, develop in about 33 days, medium-sized chinstrap and African penguins take up to 40 days, king penguins up to 56 days, and emperors about 64 days. To hatch, a penguin chick uses the sharp "egg tooth" on the tip of its beak to chisel its way out of the egg. Hatching can take between 24 and 72 hours.

47

Materials

* reproducible page 50
* scissors
* tape
* crayons, colored pencils, or markers (optional)
* paper clip

Dive Deeper!

Egg Power

Though eggs are thought of as fragile things, their domed shape helps to give them great strength, evenly distributing added weight and pressure. Let children discover this for themselves. Collect four eggshell halves. Give each a straight edge by wrapping a piece of tape around the middle and trimming off ragged edges (see below). Place the shells in a square, dome-side up on a table. Ask children to predict how many books you can place on top of the shells before they break. Then place books, one at a time, on top of the eggs. Compare results with predictions.

Making the Model

1 Photocopy page 50. Color, if desired.

2 Cut out the egg model along the solid black lines. (Use the remaining piece with the lesson on page 45.) Make sure to cut the lines that free the upper cracked eggshell from the base.

3 Fold the cracked shell halves along the dotted lines so that they cover the chick. Fold down the tab on top so it holds the egg shut, as shown.

4 Fold back the left and right sides of the model's base along the dotted lines.

5 Tape the base at the back, as shown. Attach a paper clip at the back to make the model more stable.

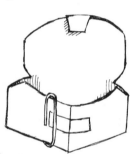

Teaching With the Model

1 What is inside a penguin egg? (a growing chick) Invite students to "crack open" their model by bending up the tab.

2 Discuss with students what's inside an egg. (a growing chick, stored food, and water) Bring in a raw chicken egg, crack it open, and show children the yolk, which is stored food for the unborn chick, and the albumen, the white part that is mostly water.

Note

As a precaution, if students handle the egg, remind them to keep their hands away from their mouths and wash their hands afterward.

Nesting Time Lift & Look

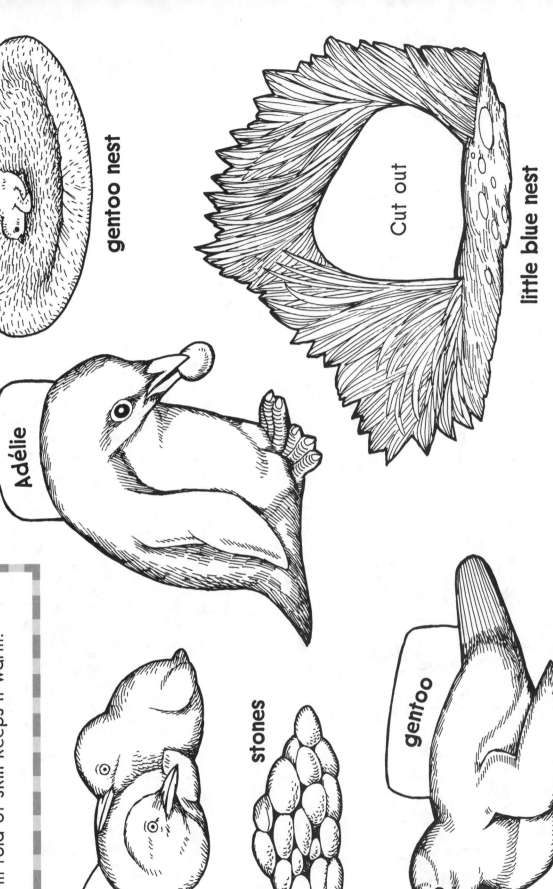

gentoo nest

Cut out

little blue nest

Adélie

NESTING TIME

Adélie penguins make nests for their eggs.
So do little blues and gentoos.
Emperor penguins hold their eggs on their feet.
A warm fold of skin keeps it warm.

little
blue

stones

gentoo

Easy Make & Learn Projects: Penguins · Scholastic Professional Books

49

Nesting Time
Lift & Look

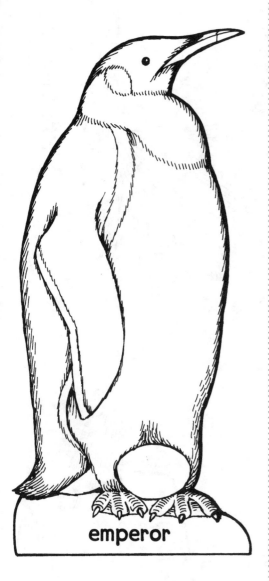

emperor

skin fold

What's Inside This Egg?
Peek & Learn

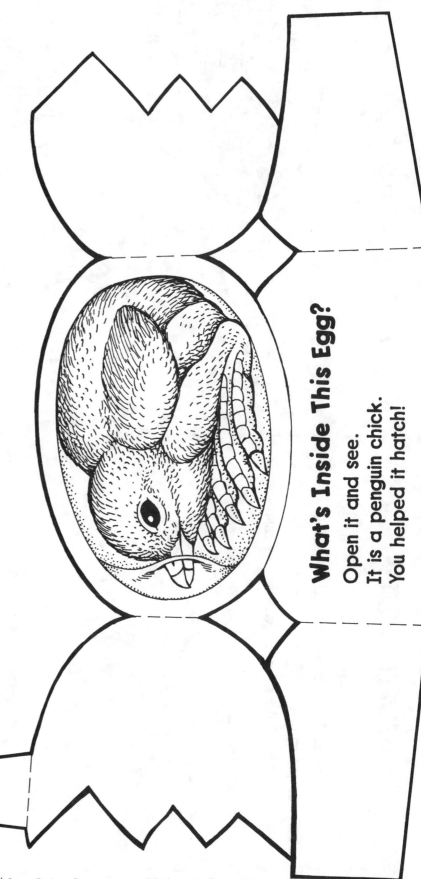

What's Inside This Egg?
Open it and see.
It is a penguin chick.
You helped it hatch!

Easy Make & Learn Projects: Penguins   Scholastic Professional Books

Please Feed Me!
Please Protect Me!

Children make a mini-poster that helps them discover how adult penguins care for their chicks.

Penguin Particulars

Both penguin parents feed and protect their chicks until they are able to fend for themselves. After a chick is born, one parent will hunt while the other watches over the chick(s). The hunting parent stores the sea creatures it catches in its crop, which is a pouch in the penguin's throat where food is partially digested. The parent returns to its chick and regurgitates this partially digested food when the chick pushes its head inside the parent's beak.

Penguin chicks face many dangers. Skuas, petrels, and other chick-nabbing birds may try to eat them. Their parents are their protectors as well as their shield from the wind and cold. After the chick hatches, one parent stands guard and covers the chick with its body. An emperor chick stands on its parent's feet, covered by a fold of belly skin.

Materials

* reproducible page 53
* scissors
* tape
* 8 1/2- by 11-inch sheet of heavy paper
* crayons, colored pencils, or markers (optional)

Dive Deeper!

Penguin Time

A parent returning from hunting at sea must find its own chick among the many in a nursery. Send one student out of the room and invite the others to gather in the middle of the classroom wearing their penguin masks. (See page 5.) Ask the "penguin parent" student to return to the room, name a child in the group, and ask the student to find that child. How difficult was it? Repeat the activity, this time allowing the "penguin parent" and the child in the group to call to each other by name. Was this easier?

Making the Models

1 Photocopy page 53. Color the penguins, if desired. Use the penguin poster on pages 11–13 as a coloring guide for the adults. The chicks are gray with black beaks.

2 Cut out the six pieces along the outer solid black lines.

3 Place the chinstrap penguin on the left side of the sheet of heavy paper. Tape it down along its bottom only. Tape the PLEASE FEED ME! text box above the penguin.

4 Slide the PLEASE FEED ME! strip under the adult penguin and the headless chick, as shown. Finish taping the penguin to the paper, making sure the PLEASE FEED ME! strip freely slides up and down.

5 Tape the emperor penguin to the right side of the paper. Tape the PLEASE PROTECT ME! text box above it.

6 Place the remaining skin fold piece over the chick so that the edges of the piece blend into the adult's body. Tape the top of the piece to the adult's belly to make a lift-up flap.

Teaching With the Models

1 Ask: What do penguins eat? (fish and other sea creatures) Where do penguin chicks get food? (from their parents) Invite children to pull the PLEASE FEED ME! piece and raise the chick's head into the open mouth.

2 Penguin parents protect their young chicks by standing guard over them. An emperor chick stands on its parent's feet covered by a fold of belly skin. Invite children to lift the flaps on their models and look at the hidden chick. Ask: What do young chicks need protection from? (cold, storms, and predators like skuas and petrels)

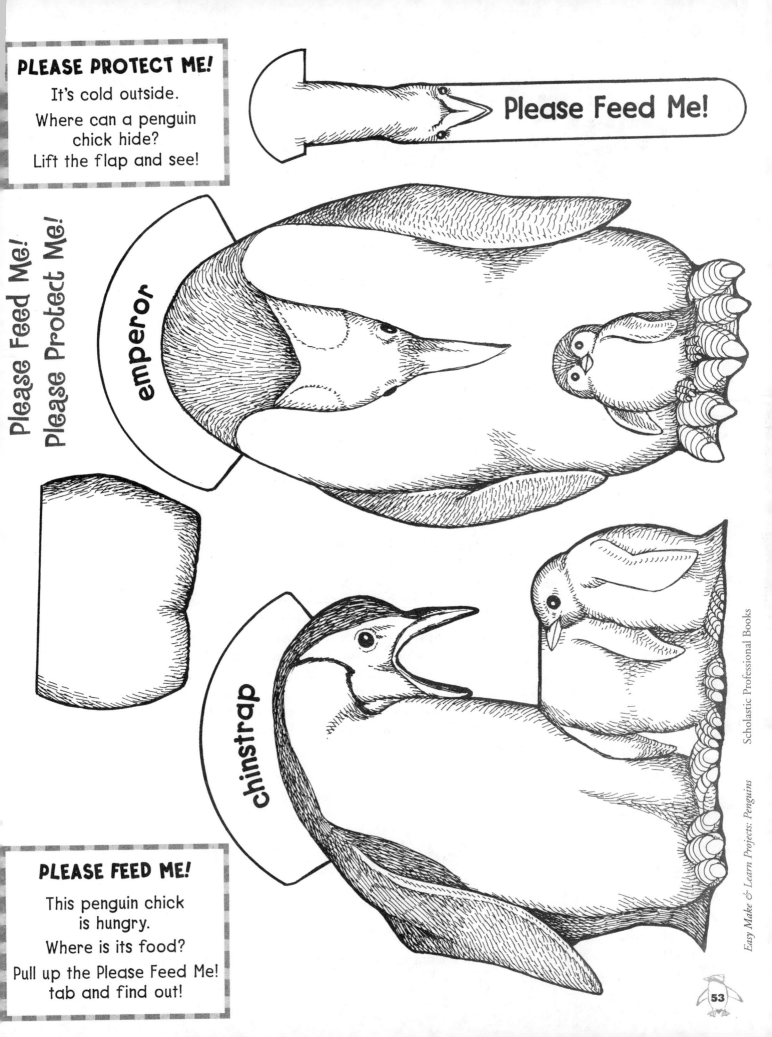

PLEASE PROTECT ME!

It's cold outside.

Where can a penguin chick hide?

Lift the flap and see!

Please Feed Me!

Please Feed Me!
Please Protect Me!

emperor

chinstrap

PLEASE FEED ME!

This penguin chick is hungry.

Where is its food?

Pull up the Please Feed Me! tab and find out!

Nursery Time

Children make a model to see how penguin chicks develop into young, independent penguins.

Penguin Particulars

As penguin chicks become larger, both parents need to hunt to keep them fed, so the chicks are left behind. Some stay near their nest burrows. Emperor, king, Adélie, and some other kinds of chicks come together in large groups, called crèches or nurseries. There may be 100 chicks in an Adélie nursery and 10,000 chicks in a king nursery. At least one adult penguin stands guard over the nursery as the chicks huddle together and wait for their parents to return with food, keeping warm and safe. Chicks find their returning parents by responding to their call. Over time, parents stop feeding their chicks, the nursery breaks up, and chicks start to find their own food. Before they can swim, hunt, and care for themselves, however, they must molt their fluffy, warm baby feathers and grow smooth, waterproof, adult ones.

Materials

* reproducible page 56
* scissors
* tape
* cotton balls
* glue
* crayons, colored pencils, or markers (optional)

 ## Making the Model

1 Reproduce page 56. Color the emperor chicks, if desired. They are gray with black beaks.

2 Cut out the single piece along the solid black lines.

3 Spread glue on the body of the chick at the far left. Cover the body with cotton balls.

4 Dot glue on the chick that is second from the left. Tear off pieces from a cotton ball and attach.

5 Dot glue in two or three spots on the chick that is third from the left. Tear off smaller pieces from a cotton ball and attach.

6 Roll the piece into a cylinder and tape it together.

Teaching With the Model

1 Ask students to count the number of chicks in their Nursery Time model. Consider having students place all their models together to make a larger nursery.

2 Explain to children that the cotton on the Nursery Time model represents the fuzzy, warm baby feathers that penguin chicks are born with. Ask students to turn their models around and around. What do they think is happening to the chick's baby feathers? (They are falling out.) Ask: How is this like when you lose baby teeth?

Nursery
Time

Easy Make & Learn Projects: Penguins

Scholastic Professional Books